These Were Your Father's

John Hegley

THESE
WERE
YOUR
FATHER'S

with drawings by the author

Methuen

First published in Great Britain in 1994
by Methuen London
an imprint of Reed Consumer Books Ltd
Michelin House, 81 Fulham Road, London SW3 6RB
and Auckland, Melbourne, Singapore and Toronto

Copyright © 1994 by John Hegley
The author has asserted his moral rights

A CIP catalogue record for this book
is available from the British Library
ISBN 0 413 68730 9

Phototypeset by Intype, London
Printed in Great Britain
by Clays Ltd, St Ives plc

Contents

A few words about poetry

Adrian Mitchell has suggested that most people ignore most poetry because most poetry ignores most people, to which I would add that most porcupines ignore most putty because putty is usually quite high off the ground and porcupines usually aren't and they tend not to notice things unless they're of an edible, threatening, or sexually attractive nature.

D.H. Lawrence spoke of poetry as that which brings a new attention to something. This is what the Martian poets were after; Craig Raine, through his Martian eye, sees the book as a many-winged bird. Similarly, a pair of glasses might be seen as a bird with no wings, no body, no head and a pair of glasses.

A many-winged rain hat

Holy orders

Be sharp, be blunt,
hunt out the fox
of your own vox popular,
be jocular, be ocular
however much they mocular;
be rigorous, irregular
but don't go being negular,
whip away the rugular
from being smugly smugular,
when going for the jugular
refrain from being ugular:
enlighten and surprise,
put a sparkle in their eyes
and a few quid in your pocket.

Brother Trevor

He handed in his cowl
and his trowel
and took leave of his order for ever,
taking a position as a warder
in an already overcrowded prison.
After the celibate years
being thought of as 'a screw'
took a bit of getting used to
and in spite of having no cell of his own now
he found the new uniform didn't allow
quite as much freedom of movement.

Network SouthEast beast

Benevolent
not malevolent;
after its feast
of commuters,
they are released.

Vision in the tunnel

When you're going through a tunnel on a train
and you look at the wall
it can seem like you're going the other way
and if you want to you can go into a sort of dream
and tell yourself
that you really are
and when you come out of the tunnel again
you can feel your brain having a little problem
sorting itself out
but you may think you have enough problems already
without worrying about this sort of nonsense.

Consideration

In the crowded compartment
there's a man with a noisy computer game toy.
I'm sure it's not just me he's annoying
but I don't want to confront him alone.
Maybe I should stand up and ask
if anyone else would like him to stop
but maybe they won't answer,
and maybe they'll all take out one of their own.

Stimulation

The first time my brother saw me in action
he explained that he didn't use his hands at all
and demonstrated how he could achieve excitement
by merely rubbing his knees together.
I copied his method
as I copied many things my brother did
believing him to be a most exemplary boy
but on this occasion my only reward
was a slight abrasion of the knees.

Was it a coincidence?

Once, I'd chopped up some wood
and afterwards
in the immediate vicinity
I found some wood which had
recently been chopped up.

Light sleep

Early in the evening I like to have a kip
and dip
into the pool of the communal unconscious;
resting, passive,
where whatever size of drip you are
you make the whole
more massive.

That's entertentment

While I was gone away
down to the spray
of the ocean,
leg bent
the dog went
in my tent,
it was a small wet
and yet
it meant
more to me
than all the sea did.

A three-legged friend

They have a three-legged dog
and they call him Clover
and sometimes he falls over
and if he'd have had four legs
maybe they'd have called him
Lucky.

The Cub Scout diary

One Christmas I told my dad
that my sister had scribbled on the pages of my new Cub Scout
  diary.
When he confronted her about the damage
and she pleaded innocent
I asked who did it if she never
and realising there was no other likely suspect,
assuming our parents to be above such a senseless violation,
Angela said that although she had no
recollection of the incident
the culprit must have been her;
an admission which my father felt
warranted a thorough beating.
What had actually occurred was
whilst entering my address in the diary,
which I wanted to look as neat as possible,
I had made a mistake,
crossed it out, made a mess
and lost my temper,
ruining the book
with a series of indelible markings.
When the frenzy was over
I decided that somebody should suffer for this act of destruction
and that that person should be my sister.

Father Coombes

the old parish priest shows
me the floral feast
of his front garden
pardon my ignorance Father
but what are those?
mahonia
these?
marsh marigolds
and those?
weeds
and those there?
Dicentra spectabilis
he reads
from the little lollystick thing
leaning in the mid-March air
it is spring
and I love it
growth and greenery
and bluery above it
here in winter's hinterland
and here among the blooms
Father Coombes
bollock-naked

Private hire

In the mini-cab
the driver is sneezing
and I want to say 'bless you'
but I feel he wants to keep his distance.

Money well spent

He knew he'd been done but he'd had to have it; he loved anything old to do with scouting and this book of camping hints was a real find and the stallholder knew it. Thirty quid! But he'd had the money and what was he getting for it? Beauty, antiquity, you couldn't put a price on that. The date, nineteen twenty-eight, they knew nothing of a second world war then. The book was a beautiful orange and not at all faded at the edges, the staples too were in fine condition, no additional rust-orange against the inner whiteness of the pages, but thirty quid was still steep.

There were plenty of the old adverts which he loved, because the things which they publicised were things you could no longer buy, the addresses if they still existed would have gone through many incarnations since the time of publication, yet the text knew nothing of this and innocently promised the advertised goods for a very reasonable and archaic remittance.

He turned to the first page of the scouting material. Why was it he was so fascinated by scouting? He read a résumé of the Scout law: 'Trusty, loyal and helpful, brotherly, courteous, kind, obedient, smiling and thrifty, and clean in thought, word and mind.' He did not agree that all the properties listed were qualities but it was the attempt at a code for right living that attracted him and it was something the modern world disowned – well, he didn't. The Boy Scout movement might be moving towards obsolescence but the founding concept was sound enough. There was much good amongst the nonsense:

> the fetching hats,
> the wacky salute,

the knotting,
the yarns,
the alertness;
he loved it as a boy,
he loved it still.

He smelt the book and as he did so, he sniffed up the molecules
of another age and went into a deep deep reverie like a campfire
sleep and he was taken back to a Scout hut somewhere in the
nineteen twenties. The book WAS new, and now it had
returned to its own time and it had taken its loyal reader with
it. The group of Scouts in the middle of whom he had landed
were rather surprised, but their skipper had always realised that
the circles and rituals were a potent invocation and John set
about trying to do good Scout work to challenge the course of
history and the troop became his helpers and John had no
doubt in his mind that the book had been worth thirty quid.

Man and Gran united

Grandma she was walking
with her dog by the canal
when she recognised a foreign man
who wasn't an Italian,
it was Eric Cantona
he was sitting on a bench
Eric is a football star
and Eric's French.
Eric Cantona, Eric Cantona
he likes to kick the ball under the bar
Eric Cantona, Eric Cantona
Grandma's favourite footballer by far.
The dog jumped up on Eric's bench
and Eric said bonjour,
the doggie made an awful stench
and Eric he said eughh!
(but he said it in French).
Grandma said I'm sorry Eric
Eric said c'est la vie
and Grandma thought he said celery.
Then Eric spoke in English
and he asked the doggie's name
and Grandma said it's Jesus:
he isn't just for Christmas.

Where it will all end

If the crime statistics continue to rise
every act will be criminal
and all domestic visitors will be present
solely to size the place up
for the purpose of a burglary.
All street meetings
will end in beatings
and you will be asked if you have the time
only for it to be taken away from you.
Everyone will be on the fiddle ALWAYS.
All of the youth
will be morally uncouth
thugs on drugs;
all transactions will be theft,
all excursions will be alibis,
there will be nothing left but lies
and I don't believe a word of it.
Here, where's my wallet!

Over the top of the paper

I was sitting in the Sleazy Moon caff reading my paper,
happily immersed in the worst of the latest disasters,
when momentarily, I had a sensation that the news was just a
    blind,
something keeping me from finding something more sensational
and not so far away.
Taking a peek over the top of my page
I noticed that the salt, sugar, sauce, and mustard
were all clustered,
keeping away from the pepper
like it was some kind of a leper.
And on the other side of the table I could see
that my tea
was too big, far too big.

The fabric of life

There's a dye to colour a cotton plaster
a certain perky
pink
and the patch will match
some people's skin
but in many cases the mismatch shows
especially on the skin
of potatoes.

Friendship

On this ship of friends
if your heart sank
I would gladly walk the plank
and dive five fathoms
into your sea of troubles.

Deep in shallow waters

Relieving myself in the Mediterranean
it occurs to me that some of my wee
has become part of the wider sea
which triggers thoughts of individuals
who think they're really big
when really they are piddley.

Happy family

Under the sun the dog with a stick
under the dog the woman with thick hair.
Daddy's there with junior,
both have hats and glasses – junior's are small
that's about all
oh, and Father is fond
beyond
the call of beauty.

My father's footwear

Once, a skinhead in my class
came round my house in his Doctor Martens
and passing the rubber galoshes
which my dad wore
to dig the garden
he got me to try them on
and he said 'gosh John,
those galoshes look really smart,
you should start
wearing them into school.'
And foolishly I did.

Valentine's complaint

Apparently the Romans beheaded Saint Valentine for his
Christian beliefs, but before his slaughter he sent a message
to his jailer's daughter who'd become enamoured in their
meetings when she'd brought him his eatings.

Many times love has been declared
and many times such love has died
once it has been shared.
Love can last for ever
if we never speak its name
it seems a shame to thwart it
in a short moment of fame.
Undying loving's precious scraps
are beans we shouldn't spill
but being as I shall soon be dead
I think perhaps I will:
you've been a pal
and golden gal
to this old Valentine,
my heart is yours although my head
will shortly not be mine.
I trust the one I'm off to meet
is equally divine.

Inspector Nostril

To him the faintest odour
has a really pungent reek – I speak of Inspector Nostril.
Here is his picture:

He's called Inspector Nostril
because he only has one nostril.
Known as Inspector No Nonsense
to his friends
and Inspector Nonsense to the enemy
he tends to sniff the lower reaches of a suspect
in the way that dogs do
but he gets results.
His beak
is the peak
of his powers
so to speak.

The new member

On her wedding day it rains
rice grains
and she explains
that she has joined the pudding club.

Res Romanae (Roman things)

When we were sat in Latin
the teacher used to very occasionally break the tension
of verb and noun declension
by getting us to get out
our Res Romanae books for ten minutes or so.
These were little books in which we registered
the Roman proverb and the Roman pun
and things the Romans did for fun
like swimming
and skimming flattish pebbles
discus-like across the sea,
still pretty dull
but we got by
a little better
with Res Romanae – Roman things.

On the long last day of a summer term
the heat indoors made the pupils squirm
and the teacher who was very firm
softened up for once and said
today we shall do something different
and eagerly we started chattin'
imagining some cricket battin' –
a pleasure he would deny,
'for the WHOLE lesson boys', he told us
'we shall enjoy our Res Romanae.'

The Roman teacher

In the Greek lesson
it is the summertime
and this morning is the last time
for two cycles of the moon
that he will commune with his pupils.
Earlier this morning was the last time ever
he would commune with his belovèd
for she has fooled around with another
and his jealousy is stronger than his love.
On his arrival some of the pupils are winking at each other
thinking that today they will be schooled
without the usual iron glove,
allowed along to the beach
to have a smashing splashing time
swimming and skimming flattish pebbles
discus-like across the sea
but they are wrong.
It is *his* curriculum, *his* anger
and this morning they will share his pain,
they will each take out their tablets
and have a stab at giving six good reasons
why they shouldn't get a thorough thrashing with his cane.

On Hadrian's Wall

I imagined local children had a bladder just for kicks;
I could see them booting their ball about
down the centuries
and up against the bricks.

Wheelchairs in ancient Rome

Did they lack appropriate access?
Did the stacked steps
consistently cause despair?

Not if yours was the Emperor's wheelchair.

No credit

People know Bruce Forsyth
from the *Generation Game*,
but the rest of the participants
are more difficult to name.

The pyramids are a wonder
but we're left to wonder who
the brickies were who did the job,
there must have been a few
of them, mustn't there?

And the Bible names the wiseguys
with the frankincense and myrrh
but who knows who
the shepherds were?

They didn't get a credit.
They got lost in the edit.

Egg cosy

Before its head is splitted
the egg is fitted
with knittedness,
before the silver smash
a moment's fashion
consciousness.

Fireside fun

When we had an open fire
my dad used to hate
me sitting in the fireplace
or the grate as he would refer to it.
He used to say he couldn't feel the benefit
of the fire
but one day I made a pledge
to stay out on the edge
and the room was decorated with smiles
as I demonstrated how I could keep within the confines
of the first half-dozen tiles
and won over by the humour
my father made them mine
and in the future he referred to them
as John's six squares
and sometimes he allowed me
to have nine.

Hospital art

In the afternoons, between toileting
the doubly incontinent patients
and giving them their tea
there were a couple of hours
in which the staff and patients usually sat around staring into
    space.
I might have been the same after a few years in the place
but being an enthusiastic newcomer
and a student on vacation
I said hey, let's get everybody doing art!
So I got the materials we needed,
sat everyone around tables and proceeded.
They were not the most capable of artists
but together we made some things which put up on the wall
    together
really brightened up the ward.
The next day I was not working
and on my return I found the walls to be bare.
The staff nurse had torn down the pictures;
he told me they were ugly
and they underlined the inabilities of the patients.
I said that the pictures had gone
because they were a reminder
of the fact that he spent the afternoons staring into space
rather than trying to do something creative
with those in his care.
I said he was a disgrace.
I said I hope you're very proud,
but I never said it aloud.

My father's pullover

My father was older than other dads
and when I was fifteen or so
I used to call him 'old man'.
When I was younger such abuse
would have triggered prolific use
of the back of his hand
but I think he thought me too old and too big for that now,
not that he was cowardly,
I got the feeling that he was prepared
to square up to any aggressor
but a full-scale physical to-do with his adolescent son
would have given him a sense of parental failure.
I remember that in his frustration with my insolence
he would involuntarily pull down the bottom of his sleeveless
    pullover
which I would imitate
to make his frustration greater.

The young poet

The first time I wrote in verse
I was about ten,
I wrote about my den
and someone said it's like a real poem Miss
and Miss said it is a real poem, John.
I've been a poet since then.

The Weekender

I once went on what was called a Weekender in a hotel up in Grange-over-Sands. I'd seen them advertised when I was doing a show in the area. I took the train up there; it was at the very beginning of the mobile phone boom, and for the whole journey there were three separate people on and off these infernal machines and that was just at my table. To be truthful, when I say the whole journey I only mean the Inter-City part from London to Lancaster. At Lancaster I had to change to a local train on which I was accompanied by two of the mobile maniacs, whom I avoided by parking myself in a separate compartment where electronic game machines seemed to be the thing.

I object to mobile phones on trains because they are an imposition of something private in a public area, usually by people who kick up a right old stink if the transgression is the other way round.

Arriving in Grange-over-Sands I popped down into the town to get myself some condoms 'just in case', then made my way up the hill to the hotel. In the foyer there was a huge dog, a Great Dane I think, which moved about with difficulty. The person at the reception desk spoke familiarly with the dog and had an intriguing toupee. After receiving my key and Weekender welcoming letter, I took my duffle bags up the grand Victorian staircase to my room, number one-ten. To my delight I was at the front of the hotel with a wonderful view of the gardens and greenery beyond. To my dismay I discovered rather a lot of dog muck in the bathroom. After reporting my discovery I was apologetically moved to the room next door, number one-eleven, which had an equally enchanting view but from a slightly different angle. I settled down to enjoy my welcoming letter. 'Dear guest', it began disappointingly, but then the text went on less formally, inviting me for drinks with all the other guests at 6.30 p.m. Great, I thought, that's in half an hour from now.

After a quick sort-out and shower I made my way down the grand old Victorian staircase to face my fellow Weekenders. I was to discover that they were all at the senior citizen end of the age spectrum apart from two young people jabbering into their mobiles, whom I decided to ignore, introducing myself instead to a lively older woman who was talking to the hotel dog.

We got chattering and I discovered that she shared my interest in railway travel and the television programme *Blockbusters*. Our conversation was curtailed when she went up to bed at eight o'clock, but not before we had agreed to take the train to Barrow-in-Furness the following morning. For the remainder of the evening I chatted with the dog.

Upstairs I mixed up my complimentary cup of cocoa and relaxed reflectively in my complimentary armchair. It hadn't been the best birthday I'd had but it certainly wasn't the worst. It was certainly the second worst though, I argued with myself. 'Stop your moaning and turn on the telly.' I did as I was ordered and suddenly I perked up; they were advertising a new programme called *Bob's Your Uncle* and for a moment I thought this referred to Bob Holness the quizmaster in *Blockbusters*, but it didn't.

However the night saw a tall fall of snow which considerably increased my relish for the next day's outing. Dora understandably greeted the sight of the white with less enthusiasm on account of her greater brittleness of bone.

However, we made our way down to the station without mishap and happily sat reading our respective morning papers as we awaited the ten o'clock from Preston. I said to Dora that it was a very good sign if people felt relaxed enough to sit reading things together and Dora said she'd appreciate it if I didn't interrupt her while she was reading and she'd prefer it if I called her Mrs Phelps. She didn't speak to me again until we were arriving in Barrow and that was only to ask me to swap papers. Fortunately there was nothing in mine which took her fancy and we had a comprehensive look around the shops, a long leisurely sit in the caff with some books we'd purchased and a gorgeous journey back in the twilight snow, marred only by a couple of interruptions from Mrs Phelps's mobile phone.

To be continued

Tea and turps

You stepped into the café
then you sat down next to me
I'd just ordered breakfast
and you were my cup of tea.
You said pass the sugar
and you passed the time of day
I said it was lovely
although it was really grey.
I said do you live round here
and you asked me my name
then I asked what yours was
and they were not the same.
You said you painted portraits
and you'd like a go at mine
you said come up to my studio
and be my turpentine.

Pat's paintings

Who's this then Pat?
It's my father.
What's his eye doing down there?
That's his mouth.
What's this then?
That's the Oval cricket ground.
Looks more oblong to me. What's that brown thing?
My mother's dog.
And who's that oblong woman, your mother?
Yes it is.
What's her eye doing down there??
That's her vagina.

The customer's complaint

In the caff
swapping some of her spaghetti
for a bit of his moussaka
she considered what a benefit it was having a partner
when you both wanted the same two
separate meals on the menu.
Unfortunately she considered it
to be the only benefit.

Not very independent

Picking up the paper
I cannot believe the headline.
It has nothing to do
with the argument we had this morning.
Spreading through the home news
still nothing about our domestic blitz,
the bits of sport are the athletic
not the spiteful sort;
the Arts page: no art of deception;
the Science section?
nothing of the scientific reproach;
'Business' is business as usual,
the crosswords are cryptic rather than crass,
the horoscope alas
it alludes, but doesn't broach.
Finally I approach
the obituaries
and give them my attention with dread:
fortunately there is no mention
of love being dead.

Past perfection

You used to be
my cup of tea
but now you're not so hot,
you couldn't see
enough of me
but now you see the lot.
It used to be a mystery
but now it's only us,
once you were my cup of tea
but now you're more like pus.

Table talk

SALT. Just because you've got loads of holes you think you're special.

PEPPER. No I don't I just think I'm fortunate.

SALT. You do, you really think you're better than me don't you?

PEPPER. No, I've just got more holes.

SALT. You can't stop can you?

PEPPER. Look, it's just how it is. I've never actually counted my holes you know. OK what have I got, seven, eight maybe, and you've got one. But in the whole world there are millions of holes and compared to that we're *both* insignificant.

SALT. You patronising cruet. I'm leaving you for the vinegar.

PEPPER. Suit yourself but it's only got one hole.

Poetry in India

I'm in India,
feeling more secure
and less likely to get chinned 'ere.
I made friends with a steam-train fireman
who asked how long I would stay in his country.
'Two weeks,' I replied.
'Very short?' he probed.
'I'm a very busy man,' I joked.
'What is it, the work you do?' he probed further.
'Poetry!' I announced.
'Aha!' he pounced,
'Now I understand you,
my brother does the same.
Yes, very hard work:
the feeding, the cleaning, loading all the eggs on to the lorry.'

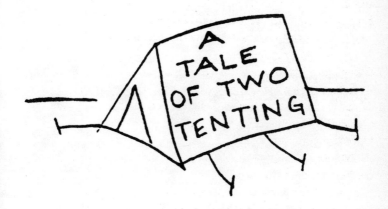

Characters

JOHN

TONY, John's friend

HERMANN, John's dog

MAJOR ROBBINGS, campsite owner

MAJOR ROBBINGS'S WIFE

BIKE-SHOPKEEPER

CAB CONTROL

GEMINI SEVEN

CAPTAIN ROBINS, scoutmaster

In the caff

JOHN. This time tomorrow we'll have tents to go to, Tony.

TONY. Two teas please Harry. You're all sorted then?

JOHN. A nice weak one for me please Harry, yeah I'm all sorted.
I'm having to improvise a bit but I'm all sorted. I've safety-
pinned a couple of blankets together. . .

TONY. Why don't you buy a sleeping bag?

JOHN. I've got a sleeping bag Tony, the blankets are my tent.
I've safety-pinned two big blankets together and gaffa-taped
some polythene sheeting to the blankets.

TONY. What about a groundsheet?

JOHN. That's what the polythene sheeting's for.

TONY. But what about the outside of the tent?

JOHN. The weather forecast didn't say anything about rain.

TONY. It did.

JOHN. Have you got an umbrella?

TONY. I've got five.

JOHN. Can I have one?

TONY. You can have four if you want. At what point do you
put an umbrella up John? You can tell a lot about a person
from whether they do it at the first tiny inkling of rain or
wait until everybody else is doing it.

JOHN. When do you put yours up?

TONY. I like to be last.

JOHN. I like to be about seventh. Are you taking anything to
read?

TONY. Just this.

JOHN. Mm . . . *The Scoutmaster's Manual*. Sounds like fun.

TONY. It says you need to take a hurricane light John, you've
got a torch on your key-ring though, that'll do.

How's the light of your love life, anyway?

JOHN. It's all over, Tone. The new beginning ended up the same as the old one. I'm emotionally derelict apparently:

TONY. How about tent pegs?

JOHN. I was going to use biros.

Hey Tone, you don't mind if I take my dog along?

TONY. What dog?

JOHN. The one made out of an old potato sack.

TONY. Bring him along.

JOHN. Here Tone, do you know how he felt when he found out that he was a puppet? . . . gutted.

TONY. No he never, John, but bring him along anyway.

On the road

TONY *and* JOHN.

We're cycling along
cycling along
singing our we're going camping song.

JOHN.

My name isn't Tony
his name isn't John
our friend's name is camping
camping's champion.

TONY.

Camping is bewitching
and it's life enriching.

JOHN.

We're champing for some camping

and itching for tent-pitching
and our camping kitching.
The wheels go round
the ground goes by,
we're going camping, why?

TONY.

Because we love it.

JOHN.

We're going camping, why?

TONY.

Because it's great.

JOHN *and* TONY.

We're cycling along
cycling along
and singing our we're going camping song.

At the gate

TONY. Hello, Major Robbings? Tony McKenna – I rang you
and reserved a spot on the campsite.

MAJOR ROBBINGS. Hello there, McKenna, well you've got the
whole place to yourselves at the moment.

TONY. Thanks.

JOHN. Thanks a lot, I'm John by the way and this is my dog.

MAJOR ROBBINGS. No dogs I'm afraid.

JOHN. It's all right he's not real.

MAJOR ROBBINGS. He's not real what?

JOHN. Not real, Sir.

MAJOR ROBBINGS. A dog made out of potato sack is still a dog of some description and dogs of any description are not allowed on this site.

TONY. That's a bit tough isn't it?

MAJOR ROBBINGS. I'm playing by the book.

TONY. Yes but who wrote the book?

MAJOR ROBBINGS. On this occasion it was me.

TONY. Which gives you the right to cross things out.

MAJOR ROBBINGS. Very irregular.

JOHN. Please!

MAJOR ROBBINGS. Please what?

JOHN. Please let me bring my dog in Sir, he won't bark or annoy the other campers because there aren't any and here's ten quid.

MAJOR ROBBINGS. Any noise though and I'll confiscate him; what breed is he?

JOHN. Sack Russell.

MAJOR ROBBINGS. Very good. Name?

JOHN. Hermann Hessian Sir.

MAJOR ROBBINGS. As in Hermann Hesse, the author?

JOHN. Yes Sir.

MAJOR ROBBINGS. No Germans on site I'm afraid.

JOHN. He's from West Yorkshire.

MAJOR ROBBINGS. Ah, my wife's heard of West Yorkshire; all right boys but any noise out of him and you'll be without a dog in your camping. Comprendo?

JOHN *and* TONY. Fully comp. Major!

Pitching camp

TONY. Do you want to pitch camp straight away or shall we get the campfire going first?

JOHN. Doesn't feel right having a campfire with no camp, Tone.

TONY. You're right occasionally John and this is one of those occasions.

JOHN. Where's the mallet?

TONY. I think it's in the trailer along with the chairs.

JOHN. Why did you bring the chairs, Tony?

TONY. Well it's not to detract from the experience of camping with extraneous domestic luxuries if that's what you think.

JOHN. No I was just wondering. . .

TONY. ALL RIGHT JOHN. Let's not fall out over this. Chair one is firewood for tonight so we don't have to go looking for campfire wood in the dark. Chair two has a hole in the seat to provide a lavatorial facility: a little tip I picked up from *The Scoutmaster's Manual*, which refers to this convenience as 'the chair of leisure'.

JOHN. Gotcha, Tone.

TONY. Good, John. Do you want to use the mallet first?

JOHN. It's not very sharp is it Tone?

TONY. That's because it's a mallet John.

JOHN.
> Knocking them in knocking them in
> knocking the tent pegs in.
> They may be only biros, but I still knock 'em in.

Hey Tone, why do you think there's so much unpleasantness in the world?

TONY. Lack of communication and lack of community and the like I'd say.

JOHN. What do you think of pub quizzes; they're pretty good communal exercises aren't they?

TONY. Not bad, not bad. I suppose it depends how much people are playing to win, rather than playing to play.

JOHN. Mm. . . I reckon the campfire takes some beating; especially as an elemental experience:

in the air
on the earth
in the presence of fire
drinking water – in the form of cocoa
and expressing the fifth element
the human element
the ability to laugh, sing and be surprised.

TONY. John?

JOHN. Tone?

TONY. Hurry up with the mallet. . .

JOHN. We could have the best of both you know.

TONY. What, you mean a campfire quiz? OK I'll map out some questions.

JOHN. What shall I do?

TONY. Do as you're told John.

The minor campfire

JOHN. It's weird how it seems destructive to burn a chair intact but it doesn't if it's all chopped up.

TONY. It would have been easier to burn as well if we'd chopped it up as well.

JOHN. So why didn't we Tone?

TONY. Because it's more memorable this way, more remarkable.

JOHN. It's a shame we had to put petrol on it to get it going.

TONY. Yes and it's a shame your tent never went up in flames as well.

JOHN. That's not very pleasant.

TONY. Sorry John, I just find your tent a bit depressing.

JOHN. But where would I be without it? You wouldn't want me in yours would you?

TONY. No – all right John. Let's get on with the quiz.

JOHN. So where would I be without it eh? Tell me that will you?

TONY. OK John, I'm glad your tent never went up with the chair.

JOHN. Thanks Tone. Isn't it great to be away from the phone Tone? Humanity's developed its machines but not itself if you ask me.

TONY. You're right John. People still don't talk to each other on the underground and 4–3–3 was the beginning of the end if you ask me.

JOHN. What's 4–3–3?

TONY. A system for playing football if you ask me.

JOHN. I didn't know that: separate worlds you see Tone we're all living in separate worlds. Back home when I let the dog out, he goes straight over the fence and rolls about in the garden with the neighbour's dog. And do you know what, I don't even know that neighbour's name. We never speak, let alone smell each other's privates.

TONY. Yes but dogs are useless at football John. Let's have the campfire quiz now, are you ready?

JOHN. Ready.

TONY. Question one. Who won the FA Cup in 1956?

JOHN. A football team.

TONY. Correct. Question two, who won the FA Cup in 1957?

JOHN. Another football team.

TONY. Correct. Question three, who won the FA Cup in 1958?

JOHN. Not a team of dogs of any description?

TONY. Correct. And question four, who won the FA Cup in 1959?

JOHN. Nottingham Forest.

TONY. Well done John, you get all the questions right and your prize is to say what's happened to the campfire.

JOHN. It's gone out.

TONY. Correct again John. Time to hit the sack.

JOHN. And time for the Sack Russell to hit the sack too. Sleep tight on the slight slope Tope.

TONY. Good night John.

Day Two

TONY. Good morning John. Here's a cup of tea for you.

JOHN. What time is it?

TONY. Quarter past six.

JOHN. What did you wake me up for?

TONY. To give you your tea.

JOHN. Good morning Hermann, how did you sleep?

HERMANN. Lying down on my side.

JOHN. Well I'm glad you weren't lying on my side, it was uncomfortable enough as it was.

TONY. We've got company John. Look it's Major Robbings.

MAJOR ROBBINGS. Yes it's me. I told you what would happen if that dog made a noise. He spoke, so I'm confiscating him.

JOHN. Fair enough.

TONY. We've got more company as well John.

JOHN. Oh yeah, who's that?

TONY. Up there, look; by the wood.

JOHN. Oh hi . . . HI, HELLO THERE! Who are they?

TONY. Dibby and Dobby from Derby, John. A bit of company on the campsite. Makes more of a jamboree of it. Toast, John?

JOHN. Yes, four slices please. So what's the plan for this morning?

TONY. Collecting firewood for tonight, putting up the campfire and cleaning our bikes.

JOHN. That's not much fun!

TONY. All right we'll clean each other's bikes and then we'll have a game of frisbee.

JOHN. We haven't got a frisbee.

TONY. We'll use a stick.

JOHN. Hermann'll enjoy that. Good dog!

TONY. He's gone John.

JOHN. Gone!

TONY. Major Robbings just took him.

JOHN. Oh . . . oh yes, I'm not quite with it. I didn't sleep at all well actually.

TONY. Why not?

JOHN. I was using my saddle and bike-lights as a pillow.

TONY. Why's that?

JOHN. To make sure nobody nicked them of course!

TONY. Who?

JOHN. What about those other campers?

TONY. You didn't know they were there.

JOHN. I did.

TONY. You never.

JOHN. I did – I intuited it.

TONY. They don't seem much like bicycle thieves.

JOHN. And they might not be. And maybe they're not whole bicycle thieves but just a little bit of someone's bike – could be tempting couldn't it, just a little bit – like a back light for instance!

Never trust someone you don't know Tony. Simple straightforward advice.

TONY. I'm going to brush my teeth John.

JOHN. What about the toast?

TONY. I've brushed that already.

In the wood

TONY. Right John, before you start chopping let me tell you what *The Scoutmaster's Manual* says about the burning properties of wood, OK?

Ash – the best of all burning woods

Beech – very good

Cedar – good

Elder – useless

Hazel – steady

Larch – good tinder but otherwise disappointing

Oak – slow but steady

JOHN. What sort of tree is this one, Tone?

TONY. No idea John, cut some down anyway and just remember

the basic rules of axe-safety: cut into the wood rather than the self and never chop a leaning stick.

Back at the camp

JOHN. I don't believe it, my doss bag's gone. Let's have a look in your tent. I don't believe it, your doss bag's gone as well!

TONY. But who'd want a couple of old doss bags?

JOHN. The other campers of course.

TONY. But they wouldn't have come camping without doss bags.

JOHN. Haven't you ever heard of extra warmth?

TONY. Yes I have actually.

JOHN. Well that's what I reckon they've gone for. Come on Tony.

Up at the other campers'

TONY. Don't be too hasty John, knock first.

JOHN. All right.

TONY. And use some discretion, please John!

JOHN. Of course. Ah excuse me, our sleeping arrangements have disappeared. You haven't stolen them by any chance have you? No? Well you don't mind if we inspect your tent then. Some other thieves might have hidden them behind some of your effects.

TONY. Look, I'm sorry you two but John's a bit upset.

. . . Share your sleeping arrangements! ? You mean lie beside you inside your tent!?!

I don't know – John? Dibby and Dobby have kindly offered to share their sleeping arrangements with us.

JOHN. Well – I don't want any hanky-panky for sure. I've had enough trouble in that department, but being as we're arrangementless the offer is very welcome to me. I'll just go and get some condoms.

TONY. Get me a couple as well while you're down there would you John. . . ?

JOHN. Hello everyone, I'm back.

Hey Tone, our sleeping arrangements haven't disappeared after all. I'm sorry you two. I remember, I had my eyes shut when I looked in our tents because I only wanted to see what I expected to see.

TONY. Why don't you come to our encampment, we've got a tent each that you could share.

JOHN. Yes, come on down.

TONY. Yes, bring that transistor radio as well if you want.

JOHN. I've got one just like that . . . hold on . . . oh you were just borrowing it, without permission, fine, fine.

TONY. Here's our tents, treat them like your own.

JOHN. We've just got to clean our bikes and have a game of frisbee with a stick then we'll be right with you.

After the night with the other campers

TONY. Hey John, Dobby's gone.

JOHN. So's Dibby.

TONY. So's their tent.

JOHN. So's yours, Tone.

TONY. At least we've still got the bikes.

JOHN. It's a shame the wheeels have gone though.

TONY. We'll have a hike into town to get some more.

JOHN. Maybe Major Robbings will give us a lift. At least they haven't touched the frisbee.

Up at the gatehouse

TONY. Hello there, is Major Robbings in?

MAJOR ROBBINGS'S WIFE. I'm Major Robbings's wife, the Major's just gone into town to sell a couple of bicycle wheels, can I help you?

JOHN. Oh, we just wondered if there was any chance of a lift into town to get a couple of new wheels for our bikes.

MAJOR ROBBINGS'S WIFE. Tut. He could have sold you his and saved you all a journey.

JOHN. But they might not have fitted!

MAJOR ROBBINGS'S WIFE. Oh they would, the other campers stole them from you two and sold them to the Major this morning.

JOHN. Oh right.

MAJOR ROBBINGS'S WIFE. Anyway, come in for a cuppa?

JOHN. Hello Hermann, how have they been treating you?

HERMANN. With creosote.

JOHN. Really!

HERMANN. And they keep calling me Sheddie.

MAJOR ROBBINGS'S WIFE. This is the living room, you two. . .

JOHN. Excuse me, have you been creosoting my dog?

MAJOR ROBBINGS'S WIFE. I beg your pardon!! . . . As I was saying this is the living room which doubles as a dog-creosoting parlour, now sit yourselves down and I'll bring you both a bowl of water.

TONY. Tea for me please Mrs Robbings.

MAJOR ROBBINGS'S WIFE. Sorry I was getting confused. Oh and I'd prefer it if you referred to me as Major Robbings's wife. Biscuits?

JOHN. Dog biscuits are they?

MAJOR ROBBINGS'S WIFE. No – ship's biscuits, very nice actually – you're in luck.

JOHN. We're not – you've immobilised our bicycles, you've confiscated our dog and you've covered him in creosote.

MAJOR ROBBINGS'S WIFE. No-no that was my husband. Try not to tar us with the same accusations if you don't mind. His life is his, mine is not. A joint bank account doesn't necessarily mean a joint life. He has done you disservice, I am offering you hospitality. We're different people. We do different things. I'll be right back with the biscuit barrel.

JOHN. OK Tone, after we've biscuited I'll go into town and get some replacement bike wheels – you look after what's left of the gear. I'd better get a cab back, what a drag. A cab on a camping holiday. Do you know what I hate about cars, Tone?

TONY. Yes John.

JOHN. Right, well make sure no one drives one over my tent, it's ours now, amico brother!

TONY. Allegro, John.

Back on the road

JOHN.

> I'm hiking along
> hiking along
> singing my not going cycling song.

In the shop

JOHN. Hello there, those two secondhand bicycle wheels in the window please.

SHOPKEEPER. Oh yes, I only just got them in this morning.

JOHN. Actually I recognise those reflectors, I think they were stolen from my friend and me yesterday.

SHOPKEEPER. I'm sorry to hear that sir; I can do you a trade discount on them and shall I call you a taxi – it'll be easier than walking back to the campsite with them.

JOHN. That's very kind of you, thanks; you can always rely on the cycling community.

In the taxi

CONTROL. Base to Gemini Seven. Where are you Gemini Seven?

GEMINI SEVEN. I'm just POB.

CONTROL. OK. Tell me when you're clear.

JOHN. So how come you're picking up in a nine-seater?

GEMINI SEVEN. That's all they had left.

. . . Look at that, do you see that, no indicator or nothing? Now I'm not the world's greatest driver. . .

JOHN. Nor is he, eh?

GEMINI SEVEN. Eh. . . No.

CONTROL. Gemini Seven.

GEMINI SEVEN. Yeah?

CONTROL. Did your last fare give you a Roman coin by mistake?

GEMINI SEVEN. What?

CONTROL. A Roman coin in the money she gave you?

GEMINI SEVEN. She gave me a fiver.

CONTROL. OK Gemini Seven, tell me when you're clear, I've got another job waiting.

JOHN. Oh look – there's a bank with a thatched roof – they're not very common, are they?

GEMINI SEVEN. Don't suppose they are.

JOHN. My dad used to like thatched buildings.

GEMINI SEVEN. Yeah? – Anyway feel free to smoke. Where are you going with those bike wheels then?

JOHN. Back to the campsite – the bloke who runs the campsite nicked them and sold them off in the town – and he confiscated the dog and covered him in creosote.

GEMINI SEVEN. Yeah? – no respect some people.

JOHN. How long have you been cabbing then?

GEMINI SEVEN. Twenty minutes, you're my second job. I think we're going the wrong way, sorry about that mate, I'll knock it off the fare.

JOHN. We should be all right. It's not that big this town, is it?

GEMINI SEVEN. It's big enough when you don't know where you're going.

JOHN. My dad got a cab once.

CONTROL. Gemini Seven. . .

GEMINI SEVEN. Hold on mate.

CONTROL. Gemini Seven: She says she definitely paid you the fare in coin.

GEMINI SEVEN. She's mistaken.

CONTROL. But she's a regular, Gemini Seven.

JOHN. Fancy that, a Roman coin; fancy someone having a Roman coin loose in their pocket.

GEMINI SEVEN. Don't you start. She gave me a fiver.

CONTROL. Gemini Seven!

GEMINI SEVEN. I'm sorry love but I'm bringing the bus back to base after this job; it's doing my head in. I wouldn't mind mate but I'm a Taurus!!

Back at the camp

JOHN. Here we are Tone, two bicycle wheels astonishingly similar to the two that departed.

TONY. A Scouter's Name John.

JOHN. What's that Tone?

TONY. It's a sub-heading in *The Scoutmaster's Manual* about what to call your scoutmaster. While you've been gone I've been thinking that we ought to know where we stand on this camp. We need it to be clear who's the troop and who the troop leader is. Troop alert troop alert!

Right John, 'A Scouter's Name: Friendly relations won't be built up if the Scouter is addressed as Mister. Some prefer Sir but others feel this is too formal. In many troops the name Skipper or Skip is favoured because it is both respectful and friendly.'

JOHN. Why can't I combine Skip and Tone and call you Scone, Tone? Or Scoppy?

TONY. How about Sceptical, John. Just skip the lip will you?

JOHN. Skorry.

TONY. OK John, I want to get an early night tonight. We're sharing tent-space on account of the theft remember.

JOHN. What about the campfire, Skip?

TONY. I've told you, I need some kip. I want to get a grip on the zip of my sleeping arrangement.

In the tent

JOHN. Hey Skip, are you asleep yet?

TONY. I'm not asleep John.

JOHN. Nor me. Hey, did you ever camp in the garden when you were a kid, Skip?

TONY. You don't have to call me Skip when we're not in uniform John.

JOHN. We haven't got any uniforms.

TONY. A uniform is more than something supplied by an outfitters, John, it's something inside the head, anyway we didn't have a garden.

JOHN. *We* did – but I wasn't allowed to camp in it.

TONY. Why not?

JOHN. We didn't have a tent.

TONY. Did you ever go camping with the Scouts?

JOHN. Not in the garden. In a field I did. I remember lying

there not being able to sleep, like now, it was the first time
I hadn't slept in the same room as my brother.

TONY. I used to sleep with *two* brothers.

JOHN. It was all right, wasn't it?

TONY. What, sleeping with my brothers? I used to tell my big
brother to put his socks outside the door because they stank.

JOHN. And did he?

TONY. Yes, but when I was asleep he went and got them and
put them under my pillow.

JOHN. When I was very small I had the same furry toys that my
brother once had. I built up a really intense relationship
with them.

TONY. What did you have?

JOHN. I had a dog, a lion and a giraffe. What did you have?

TONY. Some socks.

JOHN. What did you call them?

TONY. Smelly.

JOHN. Have you ever been scared of the dark, Tone?

TONY. Only once.

JOHN. When was that?

TONY. That time a burglar walked into my room.

JOHN. Horrible. It makes me scared just thinking of it.

TONY. And me.

JOHN. Ooh I'm feeling a bit jumpy. Do you mind if I put the
torch on?

TONY. Put it on John.

JOHN. Do you remember Jane who I used to fancy at school?

TONY. Yeah. Don't shine it on me though John.

JOHN. Sorry Tone, do you remember when you and Wojtek
held me down so she could kiss me?

TONY. Why did you struggle so much if you fancied her?

JOHN. I don't know but do you know what?

TONY. What John?

JOHN. The one thing in my life that I regret, that I never let her kiss me. I remember her hair dangling in my face.

TONY. It was quite short hair if I remember, she must have been close then.

JOHN. Oh she was close Tone. It's funny, I told Pat about it once and there was no jealousy, even though I said I wanted that kiss like I've never wanted one since.

TONY. It's unthreatening that's why; because you were kids and she wouldn't see a kid from decades ago as competition. Anyway she's left you now and you can kiss who you like.

JOHN. Yeah, but there's a lot to be said for persevering with a relationship.

TONY. How can you persevere if she's left you? You're talking nonsense now, John. Lights out. Come on.

JOHN. Ohhh Tone, I was enjoying that chat.

TONY. Skipper, John, there's a lot of work to be done in the morning.

JOHN. But you said I could call you Tone.

TONY. No, I'm in uniform now.

JOHN. Good night Skip.

TONY. Good night Patrol Leader.

JOHN. Thanks Skip.

Day Three

TONY. Troop troop alert!

JOHN. What time is it?

TONY. A quarter past five, there's firewood to be gathered John. The woodland awaits.

JOHN. What are you going to do then Skip?

TONY. I'm going to expect you not to interrogate your superior officer, John.

JOHN. Fair do's Skipper.

TONY. OK. Stand easy lad.

JOHN. But I'm lying down Skip.

TONY. Skip the quips, John, and get gathering.

Gathering again

JOHN. Oh hello Major Robbings's wife. What are you up to?

MAJOR ROBBINGS'S WIFE. Just walking the old legs.

JOHN. How's my dog?

MAJOR ROBBINGS'S WIFE. YOUR dog? I do find it funny the way people speak of owning a dog when most of them don't even own themselves. Are the bikes all right now?

JOHN. Yes, but no thanks to your husband.

MAJOR ROBBINGS'S WIFE. I did explain that my husband's business is his own.

JOHN. I've accepted that.

MAJOR ROBBINGS'S WIFE. But you still seem to assume that I share responsibility for him, don't you? I don't. And nor do I desire him.

JOHN. That's no business of mine.

MAJOR ROBBINGS'S WIFE. Everybody's business is everybody else's. Especially in this case because I want to share your sleeping bag, John.

JOHN. That's a bit personal, isn't it? What would your husband think?

MAJOR ROBBINGS'S WIFE. I don't know; hold on I'll call him on the portable and find out . . . hello Roger . . . I'm with one of the campers . . . the one who brought the dog . . . yes that's right, the bloke with the dodgy eyesight . . . he wants to know what you think about my desire to get inside his sleeping bag . . . yes . . . yes . . . OK thanks Rodge I'll tell him.

He says he thinks you're obsessed with ownership. And for once he's right, YOUR dog MY husband HIS wife. . .

JOHN. But they *were* OUR saddle bags he had off us.

MAJOR ROBBINGS'S WIFE. Don't you mean bicycle wheels?

JOHN. Yes, I do mean bicycle wheels but I felt like saying saddle bags. You criticise my obsession with ownership but you are obsessed with a world correctly labelled.

MAJOR ROBBINGS'S WIFE. I think you're probably better off in your sleeping bag on your own John. You're afraid of something aren't you?

JOHN. Yes, getting burgled,
        getting covered in creosote,
        getting poked in the eye with an umbrella. . .

MAJOR ROBBINGS'S WIFE. . . . . getting emotionally involved in someone else's life.

JOHN. Breaking the zip on my sleeping bag. . .

MAJOR ROBBINGS'S WIFE. All right John, I'm-a-going, any message for the dog?

JOHN. Yes. Bite.

After the second gathering

TONY. Put it down over there, over there in that rectangle I've marked out with string, that's to be the wood area. Things have got to change around here John.

JOHN. I've just met Major Robbings's wife, Tone.

TONY. SKIPPER!

JOHN. Don't you want to hear about it?

TONY. Don't you want to hear about it, SKIPPER?

JOHN. Sorry Skip, I met her in the wood and she said she wanted to get into my sleeping bag and her husband wouldn't mind. . .

TONY. . . . . I'm sorry John, I don't enjoy having to punch one of my scouts in the face, but if you're going to talk filth like that. . .

JOHN. I'm sorry Skipper.

TONY. All right lad, stand easy! OK that's long enough. Troop troop alert. Duty Patrol – latrine duty.

JOHN. But Skip we haven't got any latrines.

TONY. Yet. We haven't got any latrines yet.

Troop Two

TONY. Keep digging John.

JOHN. Hey, look! Skip, more visitors. Look Skip, it's a real Scout troop!

TONY. No more real than ours, John. Just larger. I think I'd like a word with their scouter.

JOHN. What abouter?

TONY. About a merger. Go and ask him to come and have a word, would you?

TONY. So what do you think, Captain Robins?

CAPTAIN ROBINS. At the risk of sounding uncourteous, Sir, I think you're round the bend and I certainly have no intention of putting my troop under the command of anybody else, even if they have been appropriately invested which I'd hazard you haven't. Now if you don't mind I've got some latrine-digging to supervise.

TONY. Pay no heed to him, John, he's a megalomaniac.

JOHN. Oh, can't we make an effort to be friends with them, their campfire will be the real thing, with a big pow-wow power circle and people doing turns and everything, Tone?

TONY. Skipper!

JOHN. It's no good, Tone. Come on let's admit what we are and make the most of it.

TONY. We're two fish in a little bowl aren't we? And if we make an effort there's a whole ocean out there for us to go and grow bigger in. Sometimes you've got to give up a bit of power to get where you want to be, haven't you. I do see. I was wrong John and it's important to be able to admit you're wrong; we should ask if we can join them.

JOHN. As long as we're part of the movement that's what matters. I'm sure he'll allow you to call him Skipper.

TONY. I'll have to swallow a lot of pride.

JOHN. You can wash it down with campfire cocoa. Come on Tony, major campfire here we come!

Packing up

JOHN. That campfire was a grand finale, Tone.

TONY. Showing them how to make a tent out of a sheet of brown paper went down well.

JOHN. Do you think so?

TONY. Mm. Added a bit of extra crackle to the crackling of the campfire John.

JOHN. Thanks Tone. I thought the best bit of the evening was when they asked their scoutmaster to do a turn and he did one about tent tidying.

TONY. What was it he said about tent pockets?

JOHN. If you have pockets in your tent you should tidy them but you don't need to bother with tidying the pockets in your trousers.

TONY. That's the one.

JOHN. Here's another biro, Tone. How was your sleep?

TONY. I dreamt about Dibby and Dobby.

JOHN. Oh them.

TONY. They were getting in a space ship and they were trying to give the driver Roman money.

JOHN. What a downer. It was great last night though.

TONY. It was a crackler, John.

JOHN. It was a crickle-crackler, Tony.

TONY. Do you think they enjoyed the pass-the-parcel?

JOHN. I think they'd have preferred the prize to have been a real frisbee.

TONY. They're glad we're letting them have the chair of leisure though.

JOHN. They are Tone, very glad. What did you think of that dance their scoutmaster did?

TONY. I don't think he needed to be naked.

JOHN. He wasn't!

TONY. He *was* in my dream, John.

I'm sorry about all that Skip stuff John. When you went to get the bike wheels I think I flipped a bit; I started remembering all this stuff with my father and I think his authoritarian streak just started coming out in me, it's weird, do you think it could happen again?

JOHN. Is that all the biros Tone?

TONY. Yeah.

JOHN. Rightyho let's go and get the dog.

On the way out

JOHN. Well, Major, we're all packed up.

TONY. And we're ready for the off.

JOHN. Where's your other half?

MAJOR ROBBINGS. You mean Major Robbings's wife?

JOHN. No, I mean your shadow, where is it?

MAJOR ROBBINGS. It's in the shed.

MAJOR ROBBINGS'S WIFE. Hello lads, ready for the off are you?

TONY. Ah Major Robbings's wife, good morning, we're all ready for the off.

MAJOR ROBBINGS. Please don't swing on the gate.

JOHN. Why not? You sold off our property just for a few quid that you didn't even need. You betrayed our trust. . .

MAJOR ROBBINGS'S WIFE. You're not still going on about that are you?

MAJOR ROBBINGS. Forget all that. Come on in for a bowl of water.

JOHN. We've just come for the dog.

MAJOR ROBBINGS. Sheddie? I've put him out in the shed. He's in among the pile of hessian sacks we use for our potatoes.

JOHN. He was called Hermann when I left him.

MAJOR ROBBINGS'S WIFE. YOU give him a name and that's it, is it? No one else can give the dog a name that they think's more suitable?

MAJOR ROBBINGS. Relax, darling, relax. Look I'm sorry about the bicycle wheels you boys, no excuse for it, I admit I was wrong – and I'm sorry.

TONY. Well at least that's something John.

MAJOR ROBBINGS. And before you go I'd just like to throw your sleeping bags into the river.

JOHN. What?

MAJOR ROBBINGS'S WIFE. He doesn't mean with you in them, stupid!

TONY. We've no time I'm afraid, we're ready for the off. Why would you want to do that though Major, just out of interest?

MAJOR ROBBINGS. To give you something to take away with you.

JOHN. Dirty river water?!

MAJOR ROBBINGS. Ah, you've changed your minds about the bowls of water, have you lads? Jolly good. Would you go and get the dog for them and bring my shadow while you're there, darling?

JOHN. I'll come and give you a hand with the dog.

TONY. It's not dirty river water we're having to drink, is it?

MAJOR ROBBINGS. No, just slightly murky.

TONY. Why did you put the dog in the shed? It's not bonfire night.

MAJOR ROBBINGS. I like to think of the whole of life as a firework display.

TONY. You remind me of my mother.

MAJOR ROBBINGS. Why's that?

TONY. Crazy about potatoes.

MAJOR ROBBINGS. I don't particularly like potatoes.

TONY. No, but you're crazy, though, aren't you?

MAJOR ROBBINGS. Yes, I suppose I'm not, ha ha.

TONY. Ha ha.

In the shed

HERMANN. Look at that rake – it's as thin as a rake.

JOHN. How are you Hermann?

MAJOR ROBBINGS'S WIFE. Yes, Sheddie, how are you?

HERMANN. Listen you two, do you want to know what my name really is?

JOHN. No.

HERMANN. Typical.

JOHN. Useless name. Now listen Major Robbings's wife. Have you thought about whether you're willing to give it a go with me?

MAJOR ROBBINGS'S WIFE. I thought you understood: I stupidly projected a fantasy image and fortunately had the sense to see the truth of what you were without getting involved.

JOHN. That's no, isn't it? Oh well, at least I've still got my pride.

MAJOR ROBBINGS'S WIFE. And your dog.

HERMANN. 'Ere, I'm not his dog. I'm mine.

On the way home

JOHN *and* TONY.

> We've heard the campfire crackle
> we've smelt the campfire smell
> we've been inside the countryside
> and inside our selves as well.

JOHN.

> We've been camping. Why?

TONY.

Because we love it.

JOHN.

We've been camping. Why?

TONY.

Because it's great.

JOHN *and* TONY.

We're cycling along
cycling along
singing our we're going home
from going camping cycling song.

A kangaroo dealing with some contact lenses

Something missing upstairs

This man walks into an optician's and says 'Excuse me I'd like a replacement side piece for these glasses I'm wearing.' 'But Sir, you're not wearing any glasses,' says the optician. 'I'm sorry,' says the man, 'but for a minute there I thought I was somebody else.'

Crisp glasses poem

Spectacles to me are not a fashion item;
I like to bite 'em
so I aim for a frame with flavour,
savoury if possible,
Salt and Vinegar glasses are my favourite.

Eating Bleary

Marooned,
they soon decided
that the necessary sacrifice
should be the one who'd lost his glasses,
the one they called Bleary.
They spooned him into their hunger
and the ordinariness of the meal
was eerie.

From a stable home

i

The Lord began
in inadequate accommodation:
straw instead of carpets
cows instead of dogs
and when he was a man
we aren't told
that he used his gold
to get hold
of somewhere decent.
I'd imagine he was saving himself
for his father's place.

ii *A chrimerick*

He started his life as a lad
in the worst room the innkeeper had
but the Lord was OK
'cos he knew that one day
he'd be in the big house with his dad.

This was my father

I knew him
like I knew the front of his hand.
I didn't understand his need to wallop me so much,
except that it kept us in touch.
Apart from skin and bone
I never knew
what he was made of
or afraid of,
in spite of all our time together
he was one of the strangers he warned me about
but without the sweets.

Popping into the optician's

One day John popped into the optician's and the optician said 'Good afternoon Sir, how can I help you?' And John replied 'What I need is a new pair of glasses that will indicate what people are up to behind my back. It's my sister's husband I'm talking about and I don't trust her brother either. He's a sly fox that one.' 'Certainly Sir,' said the optician. 'And will you be wanting a tint with those?'

The gaps in the furniture get her down

There was an old woman from Goole
who had a laboratory stool
and she just couldn't stand
the hole for your hand
or the bits they'd cut out of her pool table.
Other things she was unable to get on with
were the coils of nothingness in amongst the bed springs
which reminded her of the nothingness between breakfast and
   lunch
and the emptiness in some of her drawers got her annoyed
as it caused her to reflect upon her hunch
that ultimately the void was all there is.
However all this was to change dramatically
the day she bumped into John as he burst angrily out of the
   optician's.

Judith

So you're not a myth.
You're the apple of my eye
and the orange of my glasses,
you're the succulence and pith.
Judith,
be my kin,
give us a kith.

Roger

Roger's in love with the teacher
but his love doesn't register.

Please Miss, Roger's having trouble
Roger's love is true
it says so on the inside of his desk
is there anything that you can do
to rescue Roger, Miss?

He's hoping for a sign
that says 'Roger, will you please be mine',
don't you realise why he keeps on coming up and sharpening
  his pencils?
I've seen him breaking them on purpose.

He's in short trousers now
but they'll soon be longer,
don't worry about his age Miss
who's to say that just because a person's older
their love is stronger?

When you put 'please see me'
it always pleases Roger
but he'd prefer it
if you could say 'please see me after school',
maybe down the outdoor swimming pool, Miss
the other kids don't go there in January.

Miss, Roger loves you.
But not as much as I do.

Without drought

The sky is spitting a lot
even though it is not
a footballer.

Where's the
Comedy Tent?

The rain in Reading
was rodding up a flood
and there was mud
and sudden skidding.
'The Comedy Tent?'
the steward went,
'It's over there.
What's left of it.'
He indicated a large skeleton
bereft of canvas
and I asked if he was kidding.

It had gone up like a kite.
The previous night
the windy might
and the downpour's weight
were proof too great,
the roof had ripped
and the spreading had flown
as the Comedy Tent
did a turn of its own.

Glastonbury Festival field life

First night under canvas
two hours after the music finishes
the day begins,
with the sleep-shattering
aluminium clatter
of potential accommodation
tipped beside your ear,
accompanied by the natter
of those who have put away far too much 'gear'
to seriously consider these outsized spillikins.
They will have a go though
for the next two hours or so,
not knowing the difference
between a tent pole,
a toilet roll
and the megaphone they have brought along
to heckle the comedians.

The winner

In the Northern factory
it hadn't been easy
to gain acceptance,
being a student and a Southerner,
but one lunchtime
in the canteen
when one of the workers
observed that you could use
tomato ketchup to clean up old coins,
I said that it was better on your food
and the other lads congratulated me
on this piece of comedy
and I felt a stirring in my loins:
for the first time I had flirted with popular entertainment
and the lad who'd given us
the handy tip
squirted some ketchup onto
my glasses.

Spring rain

The April downpour brings
out three things:
the umbrella seller
the fragrance of pavements
and a lot of moisture.

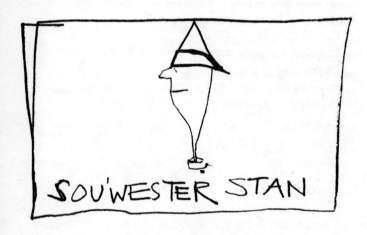

SOU'WESTER STAN

Bus conduct

After an undignified boarding,
with his can of Special Strength,
the old inebriate staggered half the length
of the crowded lower deck,
then levelled a dishevelled request
at a tidier young woman
to provide him with her seat.
Uncomplainingly she complied,
the sign said to give it up to the elderly
and social disadvantages aside
this man qualified
and after a slightly unsettling period of settling in
he was able to get on
with the business of belligerence
to persons unspecified
in relative comfort.

Wrong

I bought a one-day travel pass
and I lost it.
I got on a bus in a zone where the pass
would have been valid.
The conductor came by and didn't ask for my fare
and I thought is it wrong of me not to volunteer?
Technically I am fare-dodging.
But not in the eyes of God.

No more bus company

At the age of twenty-three
my mother sat me on her knee
and she said these words to me
she said 'Johnny',
she said 'Johnny Boy'.
Now it may not sound like much to you
but it did the job I'm telling you
and I was gone out of the door
to get myself a job down at the depot,
down in Bristol,
City and Rovers town.
There were two machines and two of us
working the omnibus,
me I was the one behind
winding the handle up and bell-ringing
and on a good day singing as well:
'hello fellow travellers
it's good to have you on
you're all very beautiful
and you can call me Johnny Boy,
hold tight, all got tickets?
Hold tight, will you move on down.'
But I'll never get my job back now
not now those Bristol buses have gone OPO.
That's One Person Operation, gives a good conducting boy no
   hope-oh.
So who's going to help you get off and on?
Who's going to hand out the conversation?

Who's going to stand in the cubby hole,
who is going to say
'hold tight, all got tickets?
Hold tight – are you all right?'

From another age

What looked like a broken window
in the phone box door
was actually a very small, lone,
levitating dinosaur.

Dark

There once was a doggie called Dark,
it was just the shadow of a dog,
a dog with no stuff,
so it was difficult to locate
when there wasn't any light in the lateness
but it was a good sort of dog to have
if you didn't have any garden.

The Lord's dog

She could jump as high as heaven.
She was the sheepdog the shepherds gave him
to help him save his flock,
the one he kept alive for thirty-three years
on one tin of God food.
You hear about the preaching and praying
but not about the Lord saying
'good dog, there's a good dog.'
Nor about all the tricks he taught her:
'walkies, walkies on the water.'
Nor about the way she barked at Pontius Pilate
and marked her master's loss
by marking out her territory
up against the cross
apostle.

A trip to the theatre

As I rambled over the ruined stage
of the Roman arena,
imagining the sword-bearing audience
of another age,
someone whose clothes looked cleaner
than mine, who must have seen a
sign that I had not
got somewhat
unreasonable:
'could you keep to the paths please,
you're setting a bad example to my son!'
Politely I explained the innocence of my misdemeanour
but inside,
my slighted pride
imagined how I might have been obscener,
or better still obscurer:
'Madam, under this world's wondrous dome
I walk where I want to
for I am a citizen of ancient Rome!'

Birthday in a Roman garden

At their meeting
she gives him a greeting
and a brooch wrapped in a colourful papyrus.
It is easily opened;
it has not been sealed with Sellotape.
He attaches the gift to his garment,
lifts his head
and feels the sea of inner sickness
as he sees on her person
the small red flower of another's passion.
'Where did you get it?' he blurts
and he hurts.
'The market in Ostia,' she replies.
'I mean the love-bite not the present,
whose is it?'
'It is mine,' she answers.
And for her intelligence he is thankful
and for her infidelity he is not.
He returns the brooch
and turns in his toga towards the sun
ignoring all of her imploring him to stay,
of which there is none.

Who am I?

A wider than average trousered cider drinker
with a spider
inside a box
and an unusual dog in her pocket.

Coming for Christmas

One year when I was at college
I rang my mum
and said that I needed to give the festive season a rest
because I was so behind in my work.
It was a lie,
I just wanted to give the festive season a rest.
I heard her call out to my dad
'he's not coming home for Christmas Bob. . .
It's the only time the family has together,' she chastised me.
'I'm sorry Mum, but this work is really important,' I defended.
'But you're only ever here for a couple of days.'
'I'm sorry Mum, I'll come home at Easter.'
'He said he won't be home till Easter,' she said off mike again.
'You've made him cry,' she said,
'he's sitting here on the step and he's crying,
I've never made him cry,
you come home for Christmas and don't upset your father.'
'But he used to make me cry all the time when I was a boy.'
'Did he?'
'You know he did Mum.'
'All the more reason for you to come home then,'
she said, trying a more absurdist ploy.

The brief reunion (La réunion brève)

In spite of all the beatings
and the bile
the thing I most remember about my father
is the smile he wore
the time he saw
his Parisian mother for the first time
in seventeen years
and I heard him talk his first language
for the first time in my life
and the tears flowed down their faces
as they nattered on like nut-cases.
She was a poor and very ancient woman
but somehow she'd got the money together
to come over and see her similarly unwealthy son.

The following morning after my dad had gone to work
my grandmother interrupted my mother's household duties
with the suggestion of an unscheduled coffee break.
When my dad came back that evening
and enquired as to the whereabouts of our visitor
my mum explained that she had had to go home early
because she was an old cow.

The return match

In my early teens
I used to go off my rocker
for soccer;
my room was chocca
block with spin offs from the game.
I supported Luton Town,
their manager was Allan Brown
and I can still name
his fourth division cup-winning line-up
but I won't.
My first professional writing job
was for a readers section
in the *Football Monthly*
for which I received a few bob
to corroborate
my team's fame.
Then I moved away to Bristol
and distance triumphed.
I tried to become a Rovers fan
but it was all over.
By the time I became a man of sorts
the sports pages held no interest for me
and Luton's entrance into the top flight
flew past unnoticed.
Twenty-five years later, asked to write
something about the team of my youth
for a fashionable magazine
I decided to return to the ground
to see if I was still Luton passion-proof.

It was January, they were playing Derby,
I had comps for the Directors' box and I felt like Jimmy
    Tarby.
Derby were the favourites,
the match began slowly
and slowly turned into a contest
and a suitable test of my attachment.
I was absorbed but not partisan.
Gradually the stars of the home side shone
and just before the interval Luton found the net.
I was appreciative but no more.
I didn't get out of my seat,
my only emotion was sadness that the gladness was really
    gone
and with half a heart I had my complimentary half-time
    coffee.
And then – ten minutes or so from the end Luton's number
    eight collects the ball on the half-way line.
I remember that this was the number my hero wore
in Division Four – Ian Buxton it was then.
I look at my team sheet. Scott Oakes it is now.
I look up to see him beat three blokes.
Incredible skill
indelible skill
I'm on my feet
he's past a couple more
and within shooting distance – just.
He can't possibly score,
a soaring shot
Great Scott
it's there

a small prayer's answer
the tears come, the years go
and I'm one of the whole
I'm part of the roar
once more.

Buzzing off with the crowd
I consider how the experience would have been intensified
had the goal been disallowed.

The Weekender continued

Saturday evening was designated in our Weekender's programme as a games evening and Mr Desk, the hotel manager, came into the lounge with a pile of board games which he placed on the table saying, 'Help yourselves everybody, be my guests.'

Mrs Phelps and I opted for the draughts and we had thirty games in all, all of which I won, although in no way did this detract from my partner's enjoyment. 'It's not the winning that counts, it's the contact with the wood,' she said, keeling over onto the parquet flooring. After a reviving cup of tea I suggested that perhaps she might like to retire. 'Yes I think I would,' she answered, 'and perhaps you might like to join me in church tomorrow morning?'

'Which church would that be?'

'The Church of Christ the Martian.'

'I don't believe I'm familiar with that one?'

'I'm the only member.'

'But where's the actual church?'

'It's in my heart.'

'How will I accompany you?'

'I'll set up a couple of candles in my room if you like.'

'What kind of service will it be though?'

'Room service,' said Mrs Phelps, for the first time allowing her comedic facility into our acquaintance.

In the chapel of Room 107 the next morning Mrs Phelps explained her denomination's thoughts on the Son of God.

'Well, originally he came down from Mars as a dog. Mary didn't give birth to him though, she caught him as he fell out of the spaceship and then put him in the manger, the same as it says in the Bible. Then one of the wise men gave him a pair of glasses which made him human. . .'

'It sounds rather far fetched to me.'

'Yes, but not as far fetched as it sounds to people who knock on your door wanting to talk about religion.'

After the room service we embarked upon a snowy woodland walk during which I collected some bits for my contribution to the Weekender Fancy Dress Finale which I'd seen advertised in the hotel foyer.

Back in the warmth of the lounge I began to sew my costume and Mrs Phelps got on with some needlework of her own as we conversed in that slightly detached way that you might do in a primary school art lesson.

'But don't you think mobile phones and computers are a sign of progress?'

'Well, in a way I do, but really I think it's progress in the wrong direction.'

'Do you really?'

'Mm. I mean, there's more human interaction in a game of hopscotch than in a computer game.'

'That's true, but there's more chalk isn't there?'

'Yes. . . What do you mean?' I said, half coming out of my reverie.

'Chalk makes a mess of the pavement doesn't it?'

'Oh right, but not of society. I think mobile phones and computer games and all that stuff isolate people; they're not really progress at all, they increase the sense of self but not the sense of community.'

'What about the sense of humour?'

'I think you'd better leave the jokes to me, Mrs Phelps.'

'I keep forgetting that you make comedy for a living, don't you John?'

'Mm. Look, what do you think of these sleeves made of leaves I've made?'

'Very nice, John.'

That evening when I knocked on her door to go down to the party, Mrs Phelps appeared with a smile and a slice of cucumber, which she described to me as Martian holy communion.

'I'm nearly ready; and I won't be needing these,' she said, taking off her spectacles and turning into a dog.

My own costume was what I described as a bloke-tree; it consisted of the leaves I'd sewn onto my shirt and plenty of brown paper wrapped tightly about my legs. Soon I was hopping happily down the Grand Hotel staircase preceded by the excited yaps and yelps of Mrs Phelps, although apparently the notice I'd seen in the foyer was out of date and there was no fancy dress party scheduled for that evening.

Please be reasonable

She heaved her dry white wine over his head
it wasn't very dry.
He asked her if she believed this to be helping matters
then went to get a cloth and said
'Why can't we just discuss the subject?
They're all very well these emotional responses
but what about taking some responsibility?'
Still she was defiant.
She likened him to a social worker.
And he likened her to a client.

Imminent death poem

goodbye sunshine
goodbye moon
I believe in poetry
I believe in life
and I be leavin' soon

Goodbye song

It's nearly time to leave you
it's almost time to go,
if you've just come in
and you're wondering if the show
is only just beginning
I'm afraid the answer's no.